Letters to a Stranger

Letters to a Stranger

THOMAS JAMES

HOUGHTON MIFFLIN COMPANY BOSTON

1973

FIRST PRINTING W

Some of the poems in this volume have previously
appeared in various magazines, as follows: *Epos:*
"Cold August." *The North American Review:* "No
Music." *Poem,* No. 8 (March, 1970): "The Chest-
nut Branch." Copyright © 1970 by *Poem. Poet
Lore,* Summer, 1972: "Laceration," "Longing for
Death," "Old Woman Cleaning Silver," "Wine."
Copyright © 1972 by Literary Publication Founda-
tion. *Poetry:* "Reasons," "Waking Up." Copyright
© 1970, 1971 by The Modern Poetry Association.
Poetry Northwest: "Frog," "Love Song," "The
Poinsettias," "Room 101," "Snakebite," "Wooden
Horse." Copyright © 1968, 1969, 1970, 1971 by
The University of Washington.

Library of Congress Cataloging in Publication Data

James, Thomas, 1946–
    Letters to a stranger.

    Poems.
    I. Title.
PS3519.A529L4   811'.5'4   73–5728
ISBN 0–395–17207–1

PRINTED IN THE UNITED STATES OF AMERICA

For my mother, 1912–1972,
and my father, 1905–1972

Perhaps everybody has a garden of Eden, I don't know; but they have scarcely seen their garden before they see the flaming sword. Then, perhaps, life only offers the choice of remembering the garden or forgetting it. Either, or: it takes strength to remember, it takes another kind of strength to forget, it takes a hero to do both.

James Baldwin, *Giovanni's Room*
(New York: The Dial Press)

CONTENTS

I

II

I

WAKING UP

I

On my right is a field of darkness.
The ants are busy in the tall grass.
I float on a lake of dark petals.

II

Waves of flesh wash over me.
I am looking into watery sky
At the bottom of an ancient well.

III

The field is flooded with darkness.
I sleep in curls of dark grass
Edged by a cloud of wild asters.

IV

A horse stands by a worm-eaten log.
It paws the dark with its right foreleg,
Cutting dark flowers in the air.

ROOM 101

Chiseled out of the dark, I lie
Under the arclight. The moths steer
Clear of my eyelids. Sun hits the door
Open at morning. Every day
My mended arms grow stiff and lean.
I come to trade my flesh for stone.

Their eyes are kind as garnets. Nights,
I crouch under this yellow eye.
It is my private moon. I dry
And harden under icy sheets.
On Saturday I watched them take
My heart. Old relic, now you tick

All night beneath my tablelamp.
The hall is full of noise. Someone
Drags his cast-iron leg. I lean
Into my moon. A girl limps
On her new toes, without a crutch.
I listen to my father's watch

Clicking against my ribs. My nurse
Is frayed behind her spectacles.
She brings me needles, gauze, and pills
That fall like little unripe pears.
She brings a plaster paste to patch
My mouth. My new stone biceps itch.

I touch one granite ear, grown hard
And resonant as a conch. Light hurts

My eyes. I trade them both for quartz
On Wednesday morning. I am made
To last forever, girded bone.
A hornet tests my sculptured skin.

CARNATIONS

The scent of carnations is too heady,
Too full of edges for me to climb to sleep.
The window's colors coil and unravel, snakes
Moving through smoke, flamily shedding their skeins.
Carnations are too pale for this faceted cut glass bowl.

Instead of all this permanence,
I would have preferred a bouquet of yellow flowers —
Buttercups perhaps, petals that might shrivel easily.
If you had wanted to ignite this room,
You should have settled for a honey jar,

Some crock shaped out of stone, with slender brushstrokes
Of pale blue buds, no other embellishment.
This bed with its sleek carved fauns disturbs me,
And looking into your eyes I see a pollen-dusted pond
Shaken with silver rings before the storm begins.

HUNTING FOR BLUEBERRIES

Like two somnambulists we entered the dawn sun,
Its plumskin flashing. I squinted at its brightness.
The sky was colorless, merely a picked bone.
A few frayed clouds dissipated downfield.
You, my little cousin, eight years blind,

Guarded the lunch basket. Down at the horse pond, frogs
Regarded us below a layer of scum.
You cried and cried because I hugged you close
And would not let you go. In your shadow-peopled head
I must have been unwieldy as a python.

The mayflies had been three months dead,
But I could see them flickering in your eyes,
Those two gooseberries. I loved to lick them clean,
My tongue grazing the broken winter field
That was your only landscape, eight years old.

My hands were two large spiders that reached your bed
Each night; all day they picked blueberries
Out of the hidden thickets by the horse pond.
In that hard morning light, moonglow to you,
We might have been two trails of marsh vapor

Imperfectly matched, dissolving in the thickets.
You found blueberries in the oddest byways —
In a vein of the hill where harebells broke and faded,
Behind a clump of oaks that held the clouds up —
Plump globes the color of the evening sky,

Frosted with dust. What colors would leap
Out of the hedges! Your mother's arms,
Riddled with tiny punctures, needled blue,
Held nothing solid as these. Their blueblack juices
Stained your small mouth like watercolor.

We found a thicket dripping its liquors down.
Drunk on the fruit, a hornet threaded among them.
They plunked like raindrops in our coffee tin,
Each rain tap punctuated with a vibrant silence.
Sunflowers cluttered the grass with burnt-out tongues.

You knelt down in the leaves. And then I saw it —
I held you close again. Confused,
You pulled away from me and went on picking,
Unaware of the blacksnake coiled in the berries,
Its eyes clouded with sun, its face a death mask.

HEAD OF DUCK

My sister fears the brightness of the cleaver.
November brought a crippled wild duck
Up to our doorstep, out of rainy weather.
My father put him on the block and struck.

She sees him beat his wings again in dreams
That reach up out of the grimy winter dark
Into her shuttered bedroom. In our rooms
We curl into the frozen winter lake

And, waking, think of Mary Queen of Scots,
Of Julien Sorel, Medusa's head,
Louis XVI bleeding in the streets,
And Herod's eyes as John the Baptist bled.

NO MUSIC

In here, a name is unimportant.
You leave it behind you like a set of dentures.
It grows so far away from you it is impossible
To mouth its syllables with any kind of conviction.
It grows mild and faded as a row of stitches.

The dead have such sweet breath.
They are entirely indifferent to their surroundings,
Too wrapped up in themselves to notice anything —
A fly investigates the pearly knuckle.
Daylight withers, effacing its muscularity.

Children die with their hands stretched out,
Reaching for something they can recognize;
They move into the dusk without even thinking.
And the old fill their lungs with it like sleep
Or the tender odors of a burning field.

Flowers brighten the edges. You grow into yourself
Till it is difficult to imagine what you are thinking.
Hands folded for the occasion, you are nearly flawless.
They have shut your eyes so that their dark alarm
Flickers behind the two white lids.

Once, I stood alone in a solid wave,
Which took my entire body in its arms.
It wrapped me like a wave of terrible sleep.
Alone down there my skin grew thick as stone.
I sank. I could not breathe the stony air.

Now you bob on a surface of white flowers —
They stand still, but seem to drift in your direction.
They are white as the palm of a hand. They tell me nothing.
You lose color as they begin to mount the walls,
Gathering their stamina like a pale fungus.

It is impossible to move in all that white.
Your face is a blossom thickening to anonymity,
Erasing its features in a surge of downiness.
One dark hand buds and loses its distinction.
The light bruises and steps out of the room.

OLD WOMAN CLEANING SILVER

I polish the tarnished silverware
While pain manipulates my finger joints.
It is the kind of pain that comes
Out of the heavy silvers of the mirror
Or the white fields at the end of December.
It is a few perfect flakes of snow
When the season is just breaking.
They strike the water and are nothing at all.

Are my hands tarnishing?
I have hung the room with watercolors —
Sunflowers in a brown pitcher,
The horse at night in a field of red clover.
But the body's silvers begin to deepen
All at once. I have watched the metal darken
In the cold mirrors of my flesh.
My bruised surfaces are needles now.

THE TURN OF THE SCREW

She died. This was the way she died:
Headfirst, grazing the surface of the looking glass.
What did she see in there? The face of Judas?
Something escaped her, winnowing the darkness —
Her eyes fell open and her tongue exploded,
Troubling the silence with a rush of vowels.

Dear Father. It has rained for seven days.
A woman is taking shape out of the rain.
Sometimes I think she is my other self.
Her dress spills moth-dust on the landing.
What is the answer? Worms pulsing in a child's face?
A small face trapped forever in the mirror,
Somewhere behind the skull, in a narrow space?

He died. Even the cobblestones were ribbed with frost.
Now his face is staining the polished wardrobe.
His gaze is slippery as an eel —
It moves between me and the children's faces,
Swiveling in and out. His body splinters like the hoarfrost,
Releasing small white sparks that enter me.

Father . . . Surely I have not died. Lighting
The candles every night, I think of you.
There is a man. His eyes keep flickering
Among the dust-motes in the morning sunlight.
They watch me when I dress. Are they your eyes?
Is it decay I want? I see you moving in his face.
A world is crumbling in the children's eyes.

Flights and drops. The children are slowly dying.
They ride a little seesaw, up and down.
Perhaps they know that I am growing stronger.
I am going up. The pond is still as glass,
Bullfrogs are tuning their bassoons for autumn.
I pare each moment to a blade of sunlight. Father?

HUNTING RABBITS IN COLD WEATHER

I

I dream that I am blind all winter.
I wake, feeling my fingers begin to redden.
The needles of the pine are sheathed in ice.

II

The darkness that brings me out into the open
Moves with me over the cold hill
Like deep waters deadlocked under ice.

III

Out on the pond's surface I grow absentminded.
A thin powder of snow drifts over the ice
Like clouds moving blindly on a hard sky.

IV

I feel the snow falling in the beech wood
Where I have found the delicate prints of feet.
Clumsily, I upset a boughful of snow.

V

The woods are full of a silence.
I breathe a scrawl of ice in my own darkness
As my gun barks, putting the whole landscape to death.

THE MOONSTONE

Who has the answer? Is it in the geranium pots,
Their little flares igniting the parlor walls?
Perhaps the stableboy has found it
In a crumbling haystack washed in drops of dew.
A filmy light moves in the eyes of horses
Whose backs are rippling in the morning vapors.

Caught in the pines, the moon is dull as pewter,
Its facets smudged with soot. A luminescence
Is loosening in a bed of gillyflowers;
A blade of frost has hooked their petals back.
The house is full of hands. Who is the thief?
Grandmotherly fingers move across a keyboard,
Peeling each spindly chord to skin and bone.

Who can resolve the puzzle? Limping Lucy?
Her body has stepped off a stained glass window,
No light behind it, flat and one dimensional.
The lady of the house is at her sewing —
Her eyes have raked the room, but they are searching
For flecks of brightness on a needle point.

Who has touched the stone? The family doctor?
Drugged all last night, his nether dreams
Were troubled with the heady scent of poppies,
Small ghosts that swiveled off. His mind has wed a blankness.
The guest in the white nightshirt . . . Is he the culprit?
He sleepwalks on the stairs, among the china teacups,
His body wavering in candlelight.

Morning has strung the grass with moony gems.
The witnesses breathe lightly, they are safe.
Where will they find the stone? At the Shivering Sand?
They will touch it in the country of their sleep.
Darkness is draining off. Here are the sun's patinas.
A day-moon tries its pulse and vanishes.

JASON

Leaving. The leaves relax, crusted brown,
Upset in the disoriented light.
Temples of gold front the afternoon.

I come in dryshod, in my mushroom-colored coat,
And lean a golden branch in the bronze vase.
I watch the impermanent green disintegrate.

Lobster-colored clouds merge and pass
On the arbor's dilapidated bones.
I raise my brush. Softly I release

A runnel of gold. Morning-glory vines
Strangle the canvas, quince goes up in smoke.
Mornings are smeared with a little fog, dead browns.

I paint the morning, its embroidered silk,
The sky's incertitudes, shut-off stars,
A few innocuous pods beginning to break.

I paint this room, the vase, strawbottom chairs,
The bedspread stitched with thin blue petals
Where I wake at dawn in a meadow of cornflowers.

I learn the lion color of these hills.
I am full of the old fear of coming home,
Stopping in darkness, under the maples.

I have sketched the soft orchard, the whorl of time.
A gold leaf skips over the hardwood floor,
And nobody minds what these dark things have become,

Fistfuls of brightness on clear water,
A handful of wafers when the season broke.
I dream of the innumerable antlers of winter,

The crude, unpainted branch. My mother and father
Walk, knee-deep in leaf of oak,
In a garden where it is always October.

II

WOODEN HORSE

All by myself I tied the braided rope
Around your gigantic neck, hoisting you
Over the garden wall. You are cold and steep:
A monolith of oak, an ice-built ship.
You contain the last gift. Embossed on your thick brow,

One carven whorl balances a star.
Wine-colored, adamant, you watch me run
Beneath your forelegs, brief as Gulliver.
Your sculptured mane, thick as a hill of fir,
Is wound with wooden fruit wiser than stone.

Your head is reared. I tap your heavy flanks
With a dry stick: you rumble like a shell
Casting its echo back. My spearhead sinks
Into your raftered belly's softer planks.
I scale one foreleg's knotty pinnacle.

Scrambling across thick withers overgrown
With oak sprouts, I approach the massive halter.
Bronze scales snap and click in a light rain;
Their cold patinas catch the cuticle moon
Which rocks in the stiff crook of your left ear.

I enter the frozen oracle of your mouth
Where swallows built a nest of wet broomstraws.
Your nostrils are a citadel for bees.
The air, stiffened to silver, vibrates with
An insect hum. I poke the angry hives.

Your time come round, the raw eyes deepening,
I share your difficult fountainhead of pain.
The indolent serpent coils in the sun.
Till now, the air was redolent with warning —
Emblems spilled from the mouth of Laocoön.

I no longer fear your secret, it is a gift.
With the alien blood flooding the tight vein,
Your eyes, once worked by sticks, contain the sun.
I find you laboring, the hoofprint soft,
No less familiar, in a wooden dawn.

THE BELLRINGER

On summer nights the belfry shakes its tongues
Down Four Hills to the village square. Such winter sounds
Hollow the dream country of the villagers.
A pale insomniac with rutted eyes,
I track sleep out of time's intemperate blandishments.

Hours drizzling down to meet me, I lie on stone,
Eyes focused on the plum-colored moon,
Brittle as a wineglass on the sky's charred linen.
Visions rise up — my sister's bonewhite wrists,
My mother dungeoned in her crooked body.

Outside the church, dogs are rattling the ashcans
And crying like broken sirens at the moon's beaker.
I think of my body making its quick ascent,
Riding the bellrope an hour before Matins
When hoarfrost gloves my fingers to the knuckle.

Sleep paralyzes force. I pace the darkened arches.
The saints have been turning to stone for a long, long time —
They stand about disguised in masks of granite,
Their faces bland as swine or the sacred host.
Moonlight squanders its wine across their smiles.

Candles pinpoint the dark. I walk among them.
Erect and astonished, they are white as fingers.
No wind can snuff them out. They are Christ's ribs,
Spindly and interred here, waiting for the angel.
When I step forward, they lattice me with shadows.

Cobbles ring under my feet on the churchyard walk.
These white tablets aren't answering any questions.
Under the stones the sleepers lie in rows,
Arms folded in exhaustion, too deeply somnolent
For the moon to splinter them to shiny bits.

I hunch down, sleepless, crouching on the battlements.
Am I a victim of my own mortality?
Stars pulse and dissolve in their distant alleys
Above the face of a gargoyle, pinched and lifeless,
As if some bird had rifled its stone eyes.

FROG

Dear love, not for a moment, not at all,
Will I accept your kiss.
The water darkens. I am safe as a tadpole.

Wind shakes the water. I dine on August's last flies.
Leaves fall like paper soldiers
From their retreat in the thickets of the oak trees.

They clutter the pond's surface, flat little cadavers.
I view them from below,
Cold-blooded, serious. My arrowroot shivers.

Late June, my skin began to toughen. How
My fingers ached!
Each knuckle formed a web. Suddenly my tongue grew

Sticky and hard. Regarding me from a silver-backed
Mirror, my eyes began
To deepen; both my thighs ballooned; I sucked

At the thick air. Now wind picks at my bones.
My voice is a creaking door.
I nibble this withered marigold, the sun.

I was not cut out to be a prince; I hear
Your voice, a china bell.
I would winter in mud, under these frozen stars,

Among the turtle shells. Dead lilies fill
My days, their mouths are red.
I breathe through duckweed as the owl calls

From his gable in the oak's dark leaves, dark blood.
Thin as any witch,
The moon comes up the hill in a stiff hood

Of gold. Rocking me in your palm, you scratch
My nose. A soft white bud,
My belly blossoms underneath your touch.

SISTER MIRIAM THÉRÈSE TAKES THE VEIL

Painting marigolds in the public garden
When I was twelve and spring was a long way off,
I saw you the first time. My brush held silky filaments.
When you raised your face, I rummaged in the flowers,
Staining the paper gold. I saw answers in your eyes.
That night I woke to pain that twisted open,
Livid as beestings on my open palms.

I was the girl in the fairy tale,
Smothered in damaged leaves the birds brought down,
And where were you? Squirming on your cross
Among the chalices, the stiffened tallow.
Mornings, my beads turned into something else —
They cracked like eggs, loosing a horde of insects
That scraped their wings against my knucklebones.

Spring came. I washed my hair in icy water —
Dry, it was a counterpane of moonlight,
Holding a milky sheen. I set the candles out
And watched a crocus pierce the frosty garden.
I steeled my body for a crucifixion,
Death in the morning. Was it your death I wanted?
Or my own body ringing in the dark?

Later that week, we eased you off the cross,
Dead as a stick, yet every vein was humming.
I wanted to crawl inside your broken flesh
And lose myself in all that frantic music.
We rubbed your thighs with musk. Your face stayed frozen.
I pressed my lips against your open palm,
Tasting the clouded-over April morning.

Today they cut my hair. It fell like loops of sunlight.
Now there's a stranger in the looking glass,
Sallow and lizardy, with enormous eyes
That hold a small, indelible pietà.
This morning I am spinning back to you.
In the season of brown leaves I'll take the wedding band,
Its quick gold vise welding me to nothing.

LUNCHEON WITH THE HANGMAN

I remember the field of snow
Where I cut the throat of the servant girl.
I left her in that rumpled meadow.

Negligence became habitual.
I grew accustomed to vulnerability.
After the minor fractures of April,

Slow convalescence, a montage of sky.
The village clock, punctual as a cricket,
Tapped the penetrable gray

I mistook for sheep, a woolly light.
I decapitated the schoolmarm after a light supper
And left her head on a salad plate.

You tell me surrender is unconditional.
Lead me to the marketplace full of this good beer.
I'll swing like the tongue of a bell.

DRAGGING THE LAKE

They are skimming the lake with wooden hooks.
Where the oak throws its handful of shadows
Children are gathering fireflies.
I wait in the deep olive flux
As their cries ricochet out of the dark.
Lights spear the water. I hear the oak speak.

It foists its mouthful of sibilants
On a sky involved with a stillborn moon,
On the stock-still cottages. I lean
Into the dark. On tiny splints,
One trellised rose is folding back
Its shawls. The beacon strikes the lake.

Rowboats bob on the thick dark
Over my head. My fingers wave
Goodbye, remember me. I love
This cold, these captive stars. I shake
My blanket of shadows. I breathe in:
Dark replenishes my two wineskins.

My eyes are huge, two washed-out mollusks.
Oars fall, a shower of violet spray.
When will my hosts deliver me,
Tearing me with their wooden hooks?
Lights flicker where my live heart kicked.
I taste pine gum, they have me hooked.

They reel me in, a displaced anchor.
The cygnets scatter. I rise, I nod,

Wrapped in a jacket of dark weed.
I dangle, I am growing pure,
I fester on this wooden prong.
An angry nail is in my tongue.

SNAKEBITE

Now I am getting light as cotton candy —
Out of the two red holes in my heel
Infinity pours, goodbye to all of me.
It was pleasant to watch my leg begin to swell;
An incredible headiness washed over me,
I didn't feel a thing. The color of a bluebottle,

The sky hit my skin like water from a pitcher.
I remember only a limber brown stick
Without any fangs, then the cool white stretcher
Where I became part of an unamusing joke
And the sun became a singular gold adder,
Which gathered its constricted shape and struck.

First I dream of wool, and then of water,
The bridge gone out under my footsoles.
Sleep eddies under everything pure as a colt's star.
These ladies in white speak a mouthful of bells.
They let the sleep rush out of me like air
Out of an innertube, smudging their white walls.

Watching milady through the wrong end of the telescope,
I suck the glass pencil at noonday.
Here is a pale horse, they say; this is his stirrup.
I ride on my own diminishing. I grow gray
In the mild contagion of my sleep.
The light spreads its thin skin and grows muddy.

They feed me through tubes and comfort me with needles.
Where are the nubile, white-winged ladies

Who populate these immaculate halls?
The young men who view me have sulphur-blue jaws
That do not complain. They bring me bottles
Of adamant, they move quietly as butterflies

And are upon me when I least expect it.
Everything I leave behind is ubiquitous,
Even the undependable broad daylight
Which grows thinner each time I raise my eyes
To watch the centuries stream from my foot
And the whole world rock backward into place.

THE STABLEBOY

At night I have a dream. The same dream
Swims back, and I am riding through tall grass
With pearls of dew clear as the glass of wine

On my father's table every Christmas Eve.
I plummet through the dark, the phantom horse
Pulsing beneath me. I am dying into that dream.

I wake in stale hay, the breath of horses
Carving slow plumes that ravel up like smoke
Where spiders leave their snarled fortresses.

Last year, when I was six, the barn caught fire.
The moon cast prisms on the snow. I was asleep.
A crackle shook my head out of the dark.

The hay was quick with thin red tongues
Babbling together, shredding all the silence —
Outdoors, the folds of snow were smooth and speechless.

Pippin was crying. Her mane was red as bittersweet.
Brightness was lapping at the sorrel's withers.
An inflammation lit the frosty rafters.

Dapple was moaning. My sleeve caught fire.
Flames licked Carlotta's legs until she screamed.
My father lifted me into his arms . . .

Nights now, I sleep among the rusty spades,
Bones of horses sweetening the August night.
My head is full of objects — lean, charred rafters,

And then the dream begins. The horse is saddled, waiting.
Trembling, I look into its eyes and see
A city burning on a winter night.

IRON MAIDEN

The door shuts by itself. And then you lose your face.
It shrivels from you like a nuptial kiss,
A ripe fig puckering. Once you're inside,
You can't escape or grope to find the bone-mask
Your father wore. It blooms with age. One day
Someone will touch it like a family heirloom.

You do not die at all, you merely thrive
On suffocation. It's a benediction.
The iron fangs shine like an edge of sunlight.
They pin you down like an exotic moth,
Suffusing every muscle with importance.
Your body drops small bits of phosphorescence:

You'll find yourself knee-deep in it
Before you learn to blink or bend a wrist —
Thick as hate, it lights your privacy,
Cleansing your pierced lungs, your ruptured tendons.
Your heart grows flat and white, a scoured saucer,
No longer sticky and intractable.

Your veins contain a lakeful of bright fluid —
Breathe, and you'll drown or vanish in its ichors
Or hang suspended like a bottled fetus.
Nothing is lost for good. Bad dreams swim back
Swaddled in bands of gauze, like cat mummies.
They shift about, a personal constellation.

And what of the brain, the love seat?
It will be shattered also, like a fragile instrument,

Its complicated networks shorted out.
Shut in its iron skull, the brain will prosper.
It will be milkweed seed, a small effulgence
Trapped though its seeds take wing, its shell crack open.

DISSECTING A PIG

I
I have kept you in a laboratory jar
Comfortable as the château of your mother.
Blind, you squinted at me from the shelf
For two whole days,
And then I hoisted you, knuckles and all,
Out of your glassed-in belly.

I delivered you into the hard light
Clean as a son of God.

II
One day, your eyes slammed shut like doors.
You were the one that never went to market.
Your snout is moon-colored. I remember the time
I watched a sow get butchered.
She screamed like a woman in labor.
I couldn't look away.

Her heart kept right on pumping its bruised pistons;
The cut throat sent a jet of red to the ceiling.

III
The sun ricochets off my scalpel
As I open your throat.
I slice you like a ham,
Inching meticulously across your belly.
You take it all in stride;
You do not even smile.

You are a strongbox broken open. Suddenly
I am aware of your valuable possessions.

    IV
Someone has filled your veins with plastic
So that you do not bleed or make a sound.
Your lungs have given out
Like two deflated life preservers.
You are full of a silence.
I move above you almost reverently.

You were baptized in formaldehyde
Before I brought you to this strange autopsy.

    V
Here is your heart, fished out of the wreckage,
Inflated, mapped with ink-blue arteries,
And not at all as dreadful as I imagined.
I will hang it on a silver chain
And wear it under my clothing like an amulet
Of humming muscle, like a crucifix.

It will tap my ribs in secret for a month
Before it turns into a thin black angel.

III

WILD CHERRIES

Beyond the cemetery fence bodies are shattered
On the public highway when the snow dissolves —
All at once their bones are packed with light,
And birds come down to shake the fledgling leaves.
I know nothing of these deaths, except the stillness
That flowers over everything the moment after.

My friend and I have shared these silences
Though we are not a part of them,
Not yet. We feed on our own loneliness,
Taking what the moment hands us, nothing more.
June fastens everything in a silk repose.
Lilacs have dropped their stars with little effort.

Nuns lie under these plain stone markers.
Asleep in their long rows, whitely established
In the center of a hunger that was never theirs,
They do no blossoming; it is impossible
To think of their bodies flaking into scars.
Pale as tapers, they don't rise after dark.

Edging the cemetery fence where dusk is gathering
Its broken strands, branches of wild cherries
Bend to our fingertips. You reach for them.
Your hands are gloved in shadow —
The red juice stains your palms
As if a nail were driven into their hollows.

I watch you eat, tasting yourself perhaps,
Some bitterness that is a part of you,

And I accept it gratefully. When you smile,
I see you dying in that single instant.
Walking back home, into ourselves, we enter
A far-off country neither of us wanted.

THE HOSTAGE

When I step out, sun cuts me like a razor,
Edging into this steep place of branches.
I trudge to a hillside where there are only dandelions
And sheep coming unstuffed like ancient cushions.
I blink and look about: no room for miracles here.
The sky is a pale gray slate with chalky smudges.

But in a vein of the hill where last year's weeds
Have starved themselves to death and only chickweed
Flowers in the broken stones, I find a car
Wedged in the bracken. A few slender feathers
Ride up and vanish. In a briarpatch of skeletons
The engine purrs in the center of the wreckage.

I step into a field of weeds so deep
It is like wading into brackish water
Yellowed with pondscum and gold filaments
That have dislodged themselves out of a brittle sky,
Out of its steely vapors. The chrome bumper gleams
And fades, fastened in its nest of rubble.

Leafshadows flicker on the damaged hood,
Reflecting bits of light. A bird might take it for another world
And perish in these reflections. I strain forward —
A boy lies broken in the driver's seat,
Broken but not extinguished, for his body holds a silence
Like the fierce moment after a match is kindled.

Why isn't he aflame? Surely his arms have turned
To wings by now, wings flaking into cinders,

His body growing slender as a fawn's.
A purple flower is clinging to the windshield,
But it is broken also. A petal slides down the glass
And flutters like a tiny, vibrant tongue.

Behind the glass his face is mottled in shadow.
The prints of leaves have stained his arms.
He lies shoulder-deep in a pool of amber shadows
Whose ripples spread and pull their thin skeins back.
I would like to wash my hands in all that darkness.
I open the door. A needle of sun intrudes.

Is this what it is to be broken? To be moored in shadow?
A gravelly echo of sheep rivets me here.
I bend to him and take him by the shoulders
But not a thing inside him will ignite,
So I take his slender wings into my arms
And say: Where has your first dream vanished now? Your dream.

THE POINSETTIAS

I have grown accustomed to the pallors of stone.
The scalloped, tissuepaper sheath disclosed
Brightness like an inflammation.

They packed me off to blackness, sleep-crazed,
Riding an armory of potent needles
Toward a dark I hardly recognized.

A clear balloon, the intravenous bottle
Bobs on its rubber string, nursing
The sting under my skin. Death-rattle,

Whimper, sob, and whine vibrate along
The corridor walls. The poinsettia petals flare,
Each a forked red tongue.

Hell is a blue light. The devil's granddaughter
Turns me on the rotisserie,
Broiling my juices to a vapor.

Light returns, a punctual mist crowding the eye.
Infection stews in a region behind my eyelids.
My veins bloom blue as the sky.

My belly stitched with a tough black thread,
I am snug as a turkey. Love is a wound that will happen.
Veteran ragdoll with split sides,

A woman coughs her stitches open
Across the hall. I count the four brown prongs
Of a crucifix. Bright petals deepen,

Collapsing on the bureau top. The dinnerbell rings,
All whiteness. I am the virgin bridegroom, white,
Chastened by these hot tongues.

The birch outside my window, in a snowy light,
Stands in a waist-high drift, austere, complete,
Essential as the edge of sleet.

WINE

I have bottles to kill.

The glass is not a ruby:
It is a mouth in itself,
Emptying its waters into me.
Its good juices wander to my heart,
Making me grow.
They put me to sleep,
Firm as a river of forgetfulness,
Kissing me sweetly into the sheets.

It is the tongue of Mary.
She is red like everything else,
Clinging lovingly to her humanity,
Fingering my hair and murmuring of tenderness.
It is like swallowing an aphrodisiac
Or stepping into a bad dream.
The infections of spring
Fasten to my mouth.
This is the time of gentleness, a flowering of organs.
I am prisoner of my own sweet juices.

Oh, Christ, you are so very far away.
Your hands are full of broken glass,
And I am too small to measure your imperfect gifts.

I drink from your slender veins.
You are falling water.
I suck at your throat,
Stroking the tender blossoms of your hands.

Your wrists flower red,
And I wrap you like an expensive garment.
I am buried with you under the hill of olives.
I sleep in your torn flesh,
In the white garments of your humility.

The moon hangs like a fruit,
A heart, transplanted, that has stopped
In the middle of love.
The branches move just outside my window,
Perforated with their simple blossoms.

LONGING FOR DEATH

I stepped out of my car door, into the black,
Searching for the rag ends of some dream.
Aware that sort of thing is useless,

I went out looking for some imperfect child
Propped on its own crooked bones
Like a set of terrible crutches.

I walked out hoping to evade redemption,
The life I wanted to lose so badly
Like an old wallet, a letter of introduction.

It is easy to surrender to the point of a needle:
It is like lying down to love
With the smell of August rubbed into your skin;

It is like swallowing your tongue,
Or learning to love the tube that nurses you
Through the monotonous afternoons of snowfall.

I wanted to marry an absence,
The sound of stars crumbling without any malice
In a corner of the universe,

The raw meat of a personal wound.
I wanted to be the witch's boy
Who helps the captive children to escape.

Instead, I managed to come face to face
With the first stretchings of a spring I never asked for,
A used-up landscape twitching its nerve ends.

I touched a branch of tiny desires
Stretching their coppery buds over a sky
Grown white and vacuous as a startled face.

I stroked a branch moving in its own life
Like the crutch of some deformed child
Breaking suddenly with improbable blossoms.

I walked into a field grown tense with longing,
Riveted with the potent needles of rain.
I stepped into a flooded meadow

Where blue flowers swayed into the open
Like a poem spoken out of damaged lungs,
An iteration, into the air I did not want.

LACERATION

I didn't want you. I wanted to be left alone,
Letting the daylight wash across the walls
Like lake water on a beach in the morning light.
I wanted to touch my stitches like a broken ladder
Or a mouth much too convulsed to speak.
Now you speak. And my wound ticks like a clock,

Getting rid of another hour,
Strangling it like a hired assassin.
You say you love me. It is no use.
Two days ago they fed me through a tube
That held me like a huge umbilical cord.
It fastened to my arm like God,

Nagging for repentance, begging for my personal guilt.
I might as well surrender to my body,
Its million tight veins wrapping me like a net.
I am too full of my own poisons
To be swallowed by anybody's love.
I wake. Infection paces at my boundaries.

I have been cut, ripped open, and I have a scar
That speaks for itself in eleven different languages.
Desire flows from it like a thick sap
At the end of an intolerable season;
And lust wells out of it. They bring me the mirror —
I am thin and unshaven and even a little handsome.

At last I can be entirely indifferent.
In this bed, surrounded by the essential seraphim,

I can ignore the obvious, I can be cruel even.
I wait for sleep, for the flash of the needle,
And the pain and the forgetfulness,
Light melting on the bowl of blue flowers at my bedside.

I do not even ask for darkness any more.
I let the nurses touch me with their cool hands
Like lake waves on an empty beach at dawn.
I will wait here, there is nothing I can do,
As the entire lake begins its movement toward me,
And let the waters claim me like a touch.

THE CHESTNUT BRANCH

There is something to be said for darkness
After all. My mother's hands
Have been full of the dark all winter.

They are hollow boats not going anyplace.
They only pull the blinds
Or gesticulate at some ineradicable star.

Now the backyard unfolds its lacy pleats,
And I bring in a white branch
Because love is the lesson for tomorrow.

Will nothing cure the brightness in these streets?
A million strange petals touch
The panes. Is it a gift of snow?

Is it making up for lack of bandages?
Is it cold, is it hot —
Will it keep, should we put it on ice?

Should my sister sew it into bridal clothes?
Is it lingerie, or just a sheet
To pull across a used-up face?

Will it brighten up the arms of chairs?
It moves. It hurts my eyes.
I am not accustomed to so much light.

It is like waking after twenty years
To find your wife gone and the trees
Too big, strange white growths that flank the street.

I will stand it in the window like a beacon —
I will find it among rubble,
Still shining after years and years of exile.

I'll place it on a casket like a bunch of carnations,
Or ring it like a dead bell.
I'll wear it like a prefabricated smile.

It will enlarge; I will set the clock
By it and watch each leaf,
Each petal make something gigantic:

Tomorrow it will bud and break —
It will build itself
A town where everyone has died of hunger.

LAMBS

Under branches of white lilac
They crop the wet grass just before dawn.
They move smokily through the half-light, smudge pots
Pulsing against a thick morning frost.
My watch glows like a small, improbable moon. Six o'clock.
I have been driving into the dark too long.

I pull to the side of the road.
I am a branch, a stone. The lambs are not aware of me.
They have been fading into the hillside
Like shadows that have peopled someone's fever
In the shut room of a dilapidated farmhouse
Where the walls reiterate a spray of honeysuckle.

They ignore one another. They are blanketed with thistles,
A little out of sorts in this shabby light.
Five or six of them are wandering through a peach orchard,
Not even aware of my personal squalor.
What stumbles from their tongues is never music;
It is the echo of a badly damaged shell.

Now they are moving by a ditch of rainwater,
Inspected for flaws in the foggy mirror.
I walk into the field, I am not afraid of them —
They scatter like the last edges of a sickness.
The sun has begun to enlarge its tawny fleeces
At the expense of no one in particular.

PEONIES

I

My nephew has brought in an armload of peonies.
They are arranging themselves in a green jar
And shatter like expensive glass

Over an inch of cold tapwater.
They spring from a source of pure darkness,
Telling me nothing of what they are.

They are not a world, they are not a looking glass
Ignorant of confession. They have no voice.
Colored with terrible innocence,

White, pink, their essences break loose,
Dispensing darkness over my mother's buffet.
They breathe. They are occupants of the house

Large enough to die or start a fire,
Leaning toward the dimly lighted sky's
Insinuations, rumor of sapphire.

II

Look how light is settling. One leaf browns.
Fold after fold of brightness
Breaks out of their icy dimensions.

It spreads. It is dimensionless —
Flake after flake, it separates like a cry.
This is the skein of winter. It has no face.

It is all white edges just beginning to gray.
It is the color of a dandelion field,
Broken fleeces, a clutter of pale shadow,

Particles at the foot of a deathbed
Gathering for a celebration.
Blossoms of snow, gigantic flakes of cold

Are flattening in the summer sunlight.
Their light pastels disintegrate in motion,
Drowning. This is the deadman's float.

III
All this red is frightening. The room is livid.
It is like opening an artery.
One tight sphere gets ready to explode —

Scarlet splatters over the buffet.
The air is wild with commotion,
My peaked wallpaper is getting ruddy.

They are opening nine torches of acetylene
Burning their way toward ultimate possession.
I am not decadent or made of stone,

I am merely part of a conflagration —
No cry, no witness but a cinder,
My body erects itself in motion

Borne lovingly out of another time,
Another place. The peonies bloom like a cancer
Eating the heart out of this room.

GOING BACK

Yes, I have known something of the dark you speak of.
I do not even remember any more
What it is like to be entirely forgetful.

I knew once. That was before the day my sister married
And I crawled into the belly of the coal bin
To water the dark with my astonishment.

Now all I can do is lend my ear to rumors,
The sun bloated, coming out of extinction, swollen
Like a tumor over the unfamiliar landscape.

I will admit I am the product of a war,
Two-sided like any other, pumped up
Out of proportion, a blood feud for that matter.

On one side is the face of my dead aunt.
Where did she go after swallowing the disinfectant
Bought to scour out the bowels of the house?

Now she is whispering at my ear, a delectable language
Poured into my head like sweet oil.
She speaks of that dark peninsula

I tried to swallow whole once,
Driving it into my body's rivers
With the hammer of my determination.

She went out of her head with pain,
Straining to deliver an empty statement
Over the white pages of the bedroom.

On the other side is an insane uncle,
Hands cupping his ears, listening for destruction,
And a great aunt who went mad on diabetes.

She gathers together again in a photograph,
A nurse in Panama wearing her white defiantly.
Those eyes drove one man to suicide

One hot night. Death whined in his ear
Like a terrible mosquito, like the yellow sickness,
A huge gold sun bulging behind his eyelids.

All this still gallops through my veins.
I have even kept something of it in my bones —
The shape of their nose, their firmly tilted jaw.

How they reached the vanishing point I do not remember.
There is no way to get back
Through this long succession of addicts

Whose guilt is my inheritance.
You have noticed I am heir to the old decisions.
No one contests the sum of such a legacy.

TWO AUNTS

When I feel the old hunger coming on,
I think of my two great-aunts,
A farmer's daughters,
Speaking into the dusk in North Dakota.
I imagine the dark baron
Riding out of their mouths,
Thick-skinned and girded
Against disaster, swathed
In cuirass and chainmail and a curse.
My hunger was theirs
Too long ago. It swims in my blood,
Groping for a foothold.
It is the dark I thrust my tongue against,
The wine and the delicate symphony
That makes my head tick so exquisitely
Tonight. My ladies,
My dusky girls, I see you
With your bustles puffed up like life preservers,
Your needlepoint rose garden,
Your George Eliot coiffures,
Your flounces gathered like an 1890s valentine.
You both took heroin.
Your father never noticed.
You sprinkled it on your oatmeal,
Embroidered doilies with it,
Ate it like a last supper
At midnight. I know what you meant.
There was always the hunger,
The death of small things
Somewhere in your body,

The children that would never
Take place in either of you.
You were a garden of lost letters.
A lust inhabited your veins.
My addicts,
The village spoke of you.
Under your parasols, two rose windows,
The world swam with color.
Riding the monotonous hills at daybreak,
You escaped the indecisions
Your blood has handed down
To me. You rode your father's spotted horses
As if they might have ferried you
Over an edge, a dark mouth in the distance.
I see you ride the black hills of my mind,
Sidesaddle, gowned in lemon silk,
Galloping
In your laced-up flesh, completely unaware
Of something I inherited,
The doubt,
The fear,
The needle point of speech,
The hunger you passed down that I
Possess.

IV

MAGDALENE IN THE GARDEN

Vessel of seven devils, I spun dreams
Out of my body's chill, its raggedness —
Where is my golden child? He steps on air,
Plummeting into grayness, the sharp distances.
The pomegranate builds a flimsy steeple,
Collapsing in the odors of this garden;
The petals wrinkle underneath my feet.
Dampness is winding me in tender scarves.

Is the flesh only a temple, or a place of bones
Where nothing solid is annihilated?
Once my body was a nest of serpents,
A sanctuary for the lame, the broken —
Love snapped those brittle turnings; all their edges
Left me for something that would nourish them.
Your hand closed on my wrist, a silver bracelet
Holding a single stone with soft blue veins.

The temple bells unloose their heavy tongues
Through mild air the color of a turquoise.
Stars eat the dark. They seem to coil inward,
Regarding me with pity, or a malice
I cannot grasp or press against my cheek.
Is the world I look for trapped forever
Behind the sky's stretched fabric,
Its silkiness a mask for my desire?

Light fleshed your body that last morning.
The garden budded. You were its first light.
Now I see you in the faces of small animals —

The worn face of the lizard hunched on stone,
Its body strung with dewdrops. In the marketplace
Honeycombs contain a tribe of angels —
The search for heaven in the swart red petals
That pierce my afternoons with quiet longing.

Tonight I think my body is a lake
Where stars drop gently and efface their lusters.
In me, they turn to stone or small, blank seraphim.
Before you left I saw you in a dream.
Fumes hurried from the cave hole. You were one person.
My silks were calm as wine in an old cup,
But I could see, reflected in your eyes,
The chalice of the pomegranate flower.

IN THE EMERGENCY WARD

I have to let you go now.
I'll wait here while they try to patch you.
I want you to know
That I have been storing up wounds also.
There is nothing to it.
But it is clear that there is no remedy
For this kind of pain.
They could not reach it with all their hands.

You see, they can only prod your lovely body
With their believable knives
Or needle you shut like good leather.
Sometimes they even recommend
A long, fine pin to hold your bones upright
Or the stout metal box
That makes your lungs purr like a motor.

As I watch you go in,
I want to stand in a field of wheat
Where the sun is breaking into flower
And feel the delicate grains blowing
Across my ankles
Just as the combine heads my way.

But my body is full of dark roads
Where it is impossible
        the last drunken derelict inside of me
        find himself.
            he is reeling by a ditch of muddy water,
            I am afraid of his terrible vertigo.

Here in the emergency ward
Everything is different.
The wounds of hurt children
Heal with a kind of vengeance.
I have watched the dark eyes of a scalded baby
Grow astonishingly blue
Right in the arms of its mother.

But now you are coming back to me,
And I see clearly that nothing is impossible.
They are carrying your body, lapped in musky leaves.
Into an ancient room
Where the stone walls sweat continually
And a fly gets lost in the alleys of your head.

SAINT FRANCIS AMONG THE HAWKS

The world revolves inside the eye of the hawk.
It is a looking glass. The sky is pale and hesitant.
Birds pivot in its blues like windblown napkins.
I am a fountain. Salt pours from my lips,
Bitter and sulphurous, igniting the winter landscape.
Inside the hawk's eye I am thin and ragged —
The dawn light fractures me to pieces.
I am eaten up, dissolving like a star.
The first sharp chord twitches below my ribs,
And then I enter the body of the hawk.

I feel my pulses surging upward,
Launching themselves into the morning wind —
I taste the gouts of sunlight, hone the air
To tiny particles of iridescence.
Christ is an instrument in my left side.
Its strings nag at my flesh. They manufacture
A symphony enormous as the ocean.
Giddy, I wheel above the frozen world,
Drunk on the music drumming through my rib cage,
Trapped in the sleek black eyes, the slippery feathers.

One morning, before dawn, I saw a hawk
Carry a field mouse into the sky.
The tassels of the weeds were splashed with frost.
Below the washed-out stars, I heard the mouse
Crying to the talons in its back,
But all I saw was brightness, a light flashing

Out of the shabby feathers of the hawk,
And then the mouse tumbled out of the sky.
At dawn, I found it in a frosty thicket,
Its body writhing on the cold white nettles.

COLD AUGUST

When two white bodies shake a room with silence,
The clock utters a trembling that deceives
The chambers of the head, the shuttered heart.
The window holds an arid breath of leaves.

They slowly taste the sharp blue bittersweetness
That breaks the body's strength. The crumbling walls
Stiffen above their desperate tenderness
As frantically before the first leaf falls

They clasp their pale hands. The fierce blue skies
Tighten within their eyes, a cold wind streams
From breath to breath. Within their silence lies
The cindered chill of intricate blue dreams.

The wind swings in and flattens on the glass,
And in the room the thick light seems too much
For their white hands, which rise and meet and pass
Like wings against the summer light. They touch.

But soon their footsteps break across the doorway,
Leaving the clock behind. They shape no words,
But force their eyes into the vicious day
Against the sudden flight of hungry birds.

LOVE SONG

Love, the gold mouth has broken open.
Stars are hard as quartz.
The moon hangs like a half-eaten melon.

The veined hives bleed in little spurts,
Then thicken. Lambskins whiten
In blue weather. I said the fountain starts

Again, sun spreads, thick and molten,
Up the hospital stairs:
The sun is merely a hot eye; it stiffens

The jaws of the dead, riding out of here
In their shut cars. The morning papers
Keep the paralytics in their strawbottom chairs.

The distance is full of grasshoppers,
Dog-eared poems, soot
Blossomed like frost, bruised plums, and old beekeepers.

On the stonebuilt gallery, through late
White buds and pain,
The newest amputee has learned by heart

His wife's last letter, brand-new lines
For an old play. His stump
Echoes calf, ankle, foot. The butchered bone

Is a wry flute. A boy limps
In his thick, plaster chest,
Armor against the enemy, the stamp

Of alien hooves. They bring him mossed
Brown jars that ferry late
Chrysanthemums on floods of amethyst.

Tonight a little girl lies shut
In the west wing. Bridelike,
She curls in her white nest for the long wait,

Victim of the poison apple. Stroke
On yellow stroke, the leaves
Splatter across her windowsill. The black

Tongue is ripening. The oak's little gloves
Assault your perfect sleep,
Queen bee, poppy, fragilest of wives.

MUMMY OF A LADY NAMED JEMUTESONEKH
XXI DYNASTY

My body holds its shape. The genius is intact.
Will I return to Thebes? In that lost country
The eucalyptus trees have turned to stone.
Once, branches nudged me, dropping swollen blossoms,
And passionflowers lit my father's garden.
Is it still there, that place of mottled shadow,
The scarlet flowers breathing in the darkness?

I remember how I died. It was so simple!
One morning the garden faded. My face blacked out.
On my left side they made the first incision.
They washed my heart and liver in palm wine —
My lungs were two dark fruit they stuffed with spices.
They smeared my innards with a sticky unguent
And sealed them in a crock of alabaster.

My brain was next. A pointed instrument
Hooked it through my nostrils, strand by strand.
A voice swayed over me. I paid no notice.
For weeks my body swam in sweet perfume.
I came out scoured. I was skin and bone.
They lifted me into the sun again
And packed my empty skull with cinnamon.

They slit my toes; a razor gashed my fingertips.
Stitched shut at last, my limbs were chaste and valuable,
Stuffed with a paste of cloves and wild honey.
My eyes were empty, so they filled them up,
Inserting little nuggets of obsidian.

A basalt scarab wedged between my breasts
Replaced the tinny music of my heart.

Hands touched my sutures. I was so important!
They oiled my pores, rubbing a fragrance in.
An amber gum oozed down to soothe my temples.
I wanted to sit up. My skin was luminous,
Frail as the shadow of an emerald.
Before I learned to love myself too much,
My body wound itself in spools of linen.

Shut in my painted box, I am a precious object.
I wear a wooden mask. These are my eyelids,
Two flakes of bronze, and here is my new mouth,
Chiseled with care, guarding its ruby facets.
I will last forever. I am not impatient —
My skin will wait to greet its old complexions.
I'll lie here till the world swims back again.

When I come home the garden will be budding,
White petals breaking open, clusters of night flowers,
The far-off music of a tambourine.
A boy will pace among the passionflowers,
His eyes no longer two bruised surfaces.
I'll know the mouth of my young groom, I'll touch
His hands. Why do people lie to one another?

LETTER TO A MUTE

If I could reach you now, in any way
At all, I would say this to you:
This afternoon I walked into a thicket

Of gold flowers that had no idea
What they were after. They couldn't hear a thing.
I walked among a million small, deaf ears

Breaking their gold into the afternoon.
I think they were like you, golden, golden,
Unable to express a single thing.

I walked among them, thinking of you,
Thinking of what it would be like
To be completely solitary. Once I was alone like that.

All the field was humming, brimming
With some brazen kind of song, and I
Thought that somehow I could disappear

Into the empty hall of your right ear,
Wandering through the slender bones of you.
But I knew that I could never let you know

That it is late summer here, that I
Can hear the crickets every evening
Hollowing out the darkness at my window,

That you have vanished into a dark tunnel
Where I have tried to reach you with my mouth
Till my mouth ran gold, spilling over everything.

Tonight I looked into your face, tenderly,
Tenderly, but I can never find you there.
I can only touch your quiet lips.

If I could stick my pen into your tongue,
Making it run with gold, making
It speak entirely to me, letting the truth

Slide out of it, I could not be alone.
I wouldn't even touch you, for I know
How you are locked away from me forever.

Tonight I go out looking for you everywhere
As the moon slips out, a slender petal
Offering all its gold to me for nothing.

LETTERS TO A STRANGER

I

In April we will pierce his body.
It is March. Snow is dust over the branches.
A pony hunches in the orchard.
I stand at the frozen mouth of the river,
Thinking of you.
In the house where you live
Frost glitters on the windows
Like uncounted pieces of silver.
Already they are preparing the wine and the bread.

II

The field is banked with purple asters
And a spill of mustard flowers.
The earth has taken on terrible proportions.
Out in an unused meadow
The wildflowers have already covered
The delicate bones of an Indian.
Bees are flying across the meadow
To a hive under the rafters of the barn.
Someone is leading a horse with crippled bones
Into the spikes of clover.

III

Alexander died this morning,
Leaving his worldly possessions
To the strongest.
I watched an empire fade across his lips.
They propped him in the sun a while,
And then three women came to scour his body
Like a continent.

I am afraid of what the world will do.
Only this afternoon
I heard two worms conversing
In the shadow of his breastbone.
I slipped out of the palace
And entered a vein of gillyflowers
On the edge of potter's field.
I will not be missed.
No one even noticed.

IV

I have been thinking of the son
I would like to have.
The leaves have all gone yellow
Overnight, wrinkling like hands
In the updraught.
I drove my car by the creek
Because I had nowhere else to go.
The milkweed's delicate closet had been fractured,
Filling the air with rumors.
Despite all I could do, the sumac
Had taken on the color of a mouth.
Tonight, I perceive the young girls
In my mother's blood
Letting their seed pass by unnoticed,
A red nativity.

V

Last night they dragged the canal
For an old man's body.
Now he is singing for a hook
Just below water level.
A branch of ice is splitting open
Across each window,

And snow is dismantling the weeds
Like the breakable furniture of a boudoir.
I have been rereading your letters.
It is too cold for a virgin birth to occur
Even in the frosty suburbs
Of a wildflower.

VI

I have learned to camouflage myself in church,
Masking my body
With the body of a saint.
Last night frost glazed the face of Mary Magdalene,
And snow rode up to the altar windows.
Before morning, the sparrows came down
To the body of Saint Francis.
Now he is upholstered in oak leaves
Like a living room chair.
This morning we are preparing a crucifixion.
I am thinking of you now.
With the velvet at my knees
And the silverware shining on the altar
And the stained glass moving out of focus
And the cross veiled in black,
I am present for the news of an enormous death.
I take the bread on my tongue
Like one of Christ's fingers,
And the wine rides through my breast
Like a dark hearse.
All the while I am thinking of you.
An avalanche of white carnations
Is drifting across your voice
As it drifts across the voices of confession.
But the snow keeps whispering of you over and over.

REASONS

For our own private reasons
We live in each other for an hour.
Stranger, I take your body and its seasons,
Aware the moon has gone a little sour

For us. The moon hangs up there like a stone
Shaken out of its proper setting.
We lie down in each other. We lie down alone
And watch the moon's flawed marble getting

Out of hand. What are the dead doing tonight?
The padlocks of their tongues embrace the black,
Each syllable locked in place, tucked out of sight.
Even this moon could never pull them back,

Even if it held them in its arms
And weighed them down with stones,
Took them entirely on their own terms
And piled the orchard's blossom on their bones.

I am aware of your body and its dangers.
I spread my cloak for you in leafy weather
Where other fugitives and other strangers
Will put their mouths together.